1, 2, MOMMY & ME

KEEPSAKE COOKBOOK

Simple Recipes for Moms and Daughters To Prepare Together

1 2 3

MOMMY AND ME
KEEPSAKE
COOKBOOK

1,2,3...Let's cook together!

Our 1,2,3 Mommy and Me Keepsake Cookbook is all about the memories made while doing an activity with our loved ones. Mommies, while working with your kids throughout this book, encourage their imaginations and let them decorate, mold, or spread the ingredients and topping to their liking! Even if it doesn't end up being the prettiest bite of food, they will remember the fun they had with you by their side. We have separated the directions to the recipes into sections for mommy and me, while some recipes are grouped together. The cutting, baking, and more difficult parts of the baking will be covered by you, Mom. The easier and messier parts will be taken over by the little ones!

We sincerely hope you enjoy this book, and see how even the most simple recipes or snacks can be made into a fun filled activity with your kids!

Enjoy!

PEANUT BUTTER CEREAL BITES

INGREDIENTS

- Honey
- Peanut butter
- Vanilla Extract
- Cheerios (or cereal of choice)

DIRECTIONS FOR MOMMY

1 Mix the honey and peanut butter, then microwave for 30 seconds.

2 Add in the vanilla extract and stir.

DIRECTIONS FOR ME

3 Fold in cereal.

4 Use a 1/2 cup measuring cup and scoop out the mixture onto a baking sheet.

5 Set the bites into the fridge for 2-3 hours, then enjoy.

WHAT WAS YOUR FAVORITE PART OF CREATING THIS WITH YOUR MOMMY?

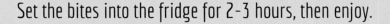

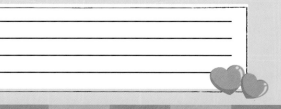

ANTS ON A LOG

INGREDIENTS

- Celery
- Peanut butter
- Raisins
- Honey (Optional)

DIRECTIONS FOR MOMMY

 1   Cut the celery into 3 inch logs.

DIRECTIONS FOR ME

 2   Spoon peanut butter into the well of the celery.

3   Place desired toppings on top of the peanut butter.

 4   Drizzle honey on top!

WHAT WAS YOUR FAVORITE PART OF CREATING THIS WITH YOUR MOMMY?

CHUNKY MONKEY BANANA BITES

INGREDIENTS

- Bananas
- Peanut butter
- Chocolate chips
- Coconut oil

DIRECTIONS FOR MOMMY

1. Cut the bananas into bite size pieces.
2. Melt chocolate chips and coconut oil together.

DIRECTIONS FOR ME

3. Create banana "sandwiches" by placing the peanut butter in the middle.
4. Dip the "sandwiches" in the melted chocolate mixture.
5. Set in the freezer for 2-3 hours.
6. Enjoy!

WHAT WAS YOUR FAVORITE PART OF CREATING THIS WITH YOUR MOMMY?

APPLE NACHOS

INGREDIENTS

- Apples
- Peanut butter
- Chocolate chips
- Honey
- Cinnamon
- Any other toppings: Marshmallows, M&M's, etc.

DIRECTIONS FOR MOMMY

 1 Cut the apples into thin slices.

 2 Spread the slices onto a plate.

DIRECTIONS FOR ME

 3 Drizzle peanut butter and honey over the apples.

 4 Sprinkle chocolate chips and cinnamon over the top.

 5 Enjoy!

WHAT WAS YOUR FAVORITE PART OF CREATING THIS WITH YOUR MOMMY?

HOMEMADE TRAIL MIX

INGREDIENTS

- Pretzels
- Peanuts
- Cashews
- M&M's
- Marshmallows
- Popcorn

DIRECTIONS FOR MOMMY & ME

1 Mix all the ingredients into a bowl.

2 Enjoy with your favorite movie!

WHAT WAS YOUR FAVORITE PART OF CREATING THIS WITH YOUR MOMMY?

FRUIT KABOBS

INGREDIENTS

- Skewers
- Strawberries
- Pineapple
- Bananas

DIRECTIONS FOR MOMMY

1 Cut your desired fruit into 1-inch pieces.

DIRECTIONS FOR MOMMY & ME

 2 One at a time, use a skewer and carefully place your fruit onto the stick.

 3 Get creative and use as many colors as you can!

 4 Enjoy your delicious treat!

WHAT WAS YOUR FAVORITE PART OF CREATING THIS WITH YOUR MOMMY?

YOGURT BARK

INGREDIENTS

- Honey Greek Yogurt
- Fruity Cereal
- Strawberries

DIRECTIONS FOR MOMMY

1 Cover a baking sheet with parchment paper.

2 Spread the yogurt over the sheet, about 3/8 inch thick.

DIRECTIONS FOR ME

3 Sprinkle cereal and strawberries over the yogurt.

4 Freeze for 2-3 hours, then serve immediately as it will begin to melt.

5 Enjoy and share your yummy yogurt bark!

WHAT WAS YOUR FAVORITE PART OF CREATING THIS WITH YOUR MOMMY?

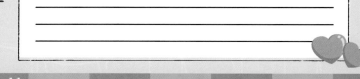

CINNAMON SUGAR PRETZELS

INGREDIENTS

- Coconut oil
- Sugar
- Cinnamon
- Pretzels

DIRECTIONS FOR MOMMY

1 Mix melted coconut oil, sugar, and cinnamon.

3 Bake at 350°F for 15-20 mins, until mixture is dry over pretzels.

DIRECTIONS FOR ME

2 Spread the mixture all over the pretzels generously.

4 Enjoy!

This will stay good for a couple weeks so make in big batches if your kids enjoy it!

WHAT WAS YOUR FAVORITE PART OF CREATING THIS WITH YOUR MOMMY?

BANANA SPLIT PARFAIT

INGREDIENTS

- Vanilla and Chocolate Pudding
- Bananas
- Strawberries
- Crushed pineapple
- Whipped cream
- Sprinkles

DIRECTIONS FOR MOMMY & ME

1 In each cup, start with chocolate pudding and bananas as the base.

2 Add layers of pudding and strawberries.

3 On top of that add vanilla pudding, crushed pineapple, whipped cream, and sprinkles to complete this delicious treat!

WHAT WAS YOUR FAVORITE PART OF CREATING THIS WITH YOUR MOMMY?

KIDS SUSHI

INGREDIENTS

- Tortilla
- Nutella
- Banana
- Strawberries

DIRECTIONS FOR MOMMY

 1 Cut up some strawberries and set aside.

 4 Roll up the tortilla and cut into bite size pieces.

DIRECTIONS FOR ME

2 On your tortilla, spread nutella over the entire surface.

3 Place a whole banana in the middle of the tortilla, and add a line of cut strawberries on top of the banana.

 5 Top each bite with a cut strawberry & enjoy!

WHAT WAS YOUR FAVORITE PART OF CREATING THIS WITH YOUR MOMMY?

PIZZA CRESCENT ROLLS

INGREDIENTS

- Crescent rolls
- Pepperonis
- Mozzarella sticks

DIRECTIONS FOR MOMMY & ME

1 Spread out your unbaked crescent rolls.

2 Add pepperonis to the dough.

3 Place a mozzarella stick in the middle of the roll.

4 Roll up your crescents and bake according to the package.

5 Share with the whole family and enjoy!

WHAT WAS YOUR FAVORITE PART OF CREATING THIS WITH YOUR MOMMY?

KIDS CHARCUTERIE BOARD

INGREDIENTS

- Chocolate sauce
- Marshmallow fluff
- Fruit
- Pretzels or Crackers
- Candy (Twizzlers, M&M's, Jelly beans, etc.)

DIRECTIONS FOR MOMMY

1 Put the chocolate sauce and marshmallow fluff into small serving bowls, and place on a serving platter.

DIRECTIONS FOR ME

2 Fill in the platter together with all your favorite goodies and treats! Get creative in the placement and don't be afraid to overlap food!

Kids will love this display of goodies for a slumber party or birthday party!

WHAT WAS YOUR FAVORITE PART OF CREATING THIS WITH YOUR MOMMY?

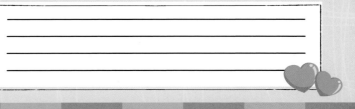

BUTTERFLY SNACK BAGS

INGREDIENTS

- Ziploc Bags
- Cheese stick
- Fruit
- Ritz Crackers

DIRECTIONS FOR MOMMY

1 Put the fruit and crackers in one Ziploc bag, but separate them on two sides.

2 Twist the ziplock a few times and tape to the back of the cheese stick.

DIRECTIONS FOR ME

3 Enjoy this awesome treat on the go!

WHAT WAS YOUR FAVORITE PART OF CREATING THIS WITH YOUR MOMMY?

GRILLED CHEESE ROLL UPS

INGREDIENTS

- Bread or Tortilla
- Sliced Cheese
- Butter

DIRECTIONS FOR MOMMY & ME

1 Spread butter on one side of the bread or tortilla.

2 Add the cheese on the side that does not have butter.

3 Cook the one-sided grilled cheese over the stove, and roll it up!

4 Dip in salsa if you dare! Enjoy!

WHAT WAS YOUR FAVORITE PART OF CREATING THIS WITH YOUR MOMMY?

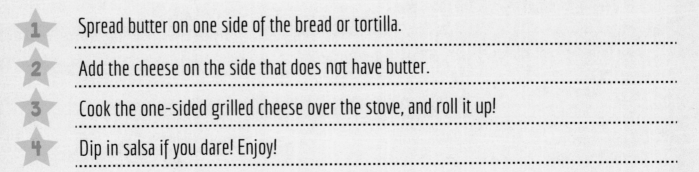

CUCUMBER SANDWICHES

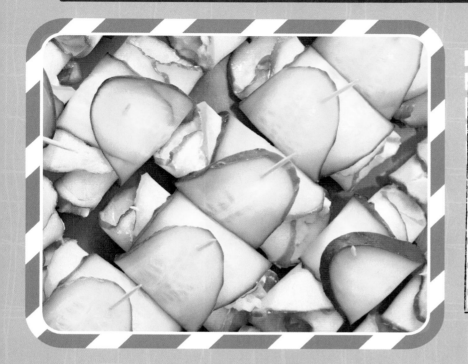

INGREDIENTS

- Cucumbers
- Ham or Turkey
- Cheese
- Toothpicks

DIRECTIONS FOR MOMMY & ME

 1 Cut the cucumbers into slices, length-wise.

 2 Place the ham or turkey on top of the cucumber.

 3 Add the cheese on top of the meat.

 4 Roll each cucumber sandwich up, and carefully place a toothpick through the center to hold it together.

 5 Enjoy your delicious and refreshing snack!

WHAT WAS YOUR FAVORITE PART OF CREATING THIS WITH YOUR MOMMY?

AVOCADO TOAST

INGREDIENTS

- Toasted Bread
- Avocado
- Salt and Pepper
- Honey or Lemon (Optional)

DIRECTIONS FOR MOMMY

1 Toast your bread to desired darkness.

2 Cut the avocados and smash them up in a bowl.

DIRECTIONS FOR ME

3 Add any optional seasonings or toppings to the mixture.

4 Top the toast with your avocado spread.

WHAT WAS YOUR FAVORITE PART OF CREATING THIS WITH YOUR MOMMY?

RANCH CUPS

INGREDIENTS

- Clear Plastic Cups
- Ranch
- Carrots
- Cucumbers
- Bell Peppers

DIRECTIONS FOR MOMMY

1 Fill the cups with ranch, about 1/4 of the way.

2 Cut your choice of veggies into long spears.

DIRECTIONS FOR ME

3 Place several veggie spears into each ranch cup.

4 Dip your treat and enjoy!

WHAT WAS YOUR FAVORITE PART OF CREATING THIS WITH YOUR MOMMY?

VEGGIE CHIPS

INGREDIENTS

- Zucchini
- Kale
- Sweet Potatoes
- Olive oil
- Salt and Pepper

DIRECTIONS FOR MOMMY & ME

1 Set the oven to preheat to 400°F.

2 Cut your choice of veggie into very thin slices.

3 Toss in a bowl with a generous amount of olive oil, salt, and pepper.

4 Spread onto the baking sheet evenly.

5 Bake for 20 minutes and flip, then bake for another 10 minutes.

Tip: If you do kale, your chips will bake much quicker. Check every 5 minutes.

WHAT WAS YOUR FAVORITE PART OF CREATING THIS WITH YOUR MOMMY?

STRAWBERRY CHEESECAKE BITES

INGREDIENTS

- Strawberries
- Cream cheese, softened
- Powdered Sugar
- Vanilla Extract
- Graham Crackers

DIRECTIONS FOR MOMMY

 1 Cut off the top on all strawberries.

 2 Hollow out the tops with a paring knife.

DIRECTIONS FOR ME

 3 Combine cream cheese, powdered sugar, and vanilla in a bowl and stir until smooth.

 4 Fill in the strawberry hole with the mixture.

 5 Top with graham cracker crumbs to complete!

WHAT WAS YOUR FAVORITE PART OF CREATING THIS WITH YOUR MOMMY?

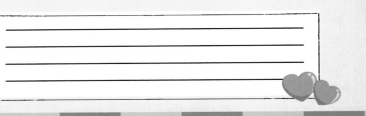

ENERGY BITES

INGREDIENTS

- Peanut butter
- Honey
- Rolled Oats
- Mini Chocolate Chips
- Chopped Peanuts

DIRECTIONS FOR MOMMY & ME

1. Combine the honey and peanut butter in a mixing bowl.

2. Then, add in the rolled oats, chocolate chips, and chopped peanuts and mix.

3. Use a cookie scooper to mold the mixture into balls.

4. Set them in the fridge for 1-2 hours.

5. Enjoy your delicious energy bites!

WHAT WAS YOUR FAVORITE PART OF CREATING THIS WITH YOUR MOMMY?

RICE CRISPY BARS

INGREDIENTS

- Rice Krispy Cereal
- Marshmallows
- Chocolate
- Coconut oil
- Butter

DIRECTIONS FOR MOMMY

1. Melt the marshmallows in a bowl.
2. Mix in the cereal according to the package.
3. Rub the butter onto the edges of a 9x13 inch baking pan.

DIRECTIONS FOR ME

4. Press the rice crispy mixture into the bottom of the pan.
5. Melt the chocolate and coconut oil then pour over the pressed rice crispy mixture.
6. Place in the fridge for at least 1 hour.
7. Cut into squares & enjoy!

WHAT WAS YOUR FAVORITE PART OF CREATING THIS WITH YOUR MOMMY?

MAC AND CHEESE BITES

INGREDIENTS

- Mac 'n' Cheese Box
- Olive oil Spray
- Mini Muffin Tin

DIRECTIONS FOR MOMMY

1 Make the mac 'n' cheese according to the package.

4 Bake at 400°F for approx. 15 minutes.

DIRECTIONS FOR ME

2 Spray a mini muffin pan with olive oil to prevent sticking.

3 Using two spoons, place a small amount of the mac 'n' cheese into each mini muffin space.

5 Enjoy!

WHAT WAS YOUR FAVORITE PART OF CREATING THIS WITH YOUR MOMMY?

S'MORES TRAY

INGREDIENTS

- Graham Crackers
- Hershey's Chocolate
- Marshmallows

DIRECTIONS FOR MOMMY

1 Line the baking tray with foil and preheat the oven to 400°F.

5 Bake at 400°F for 5 minutes.

DIRECTIONS FOR ME

2 Pop the graham crackers in half and line the whole tray with graham crackers.

3 Top the graham crackers with two pieces of Hershey's chocolate and a marshmallow.

4 Cover each marshmallow with another graham cracker.

WHAT WAS YOUR FAVORITE PART OF CREATING THIS WITH YOUR MOMMY?

BANANA POPS

INGREDIENTS

- Bananas
- Skewers
- Yogurt
- Sprinkles
- Chocolate sauce (Optional)

DIRECTIONS FOR MOMMY

1. Peel and cut the bananas in half.

2. Place a skewer or popsicle stick on the thick end of the banana.

DIRECTIONS FOR ME

3. Dip your bananas in yogurt and add your sprinkles on top.

4. Then, place each banana on parchment paper.

5. Freeze the bananas for about 2 hours.

6. Enjoy!

WHAT WAS YOUR FAVORITE PART OF CREATING THIS WITH YOUR MOMMY?

CHOCOLATE CROISSANTS

INGREDIENTS

- Croissant Package
- Hershey's Chocolate
- Butter

DIRECTIONS FOR MOMMY

1. Open the croissant package and spread them out.
4. Cook according to the package instructions.

DIRECTIONS FOR ME

2. Place a Hersey's chocolate on each piece of dough.
3. Roll up all your croissants.
5. Enjoy!

WHAT WAS YOUR FAVORITE PART OF CREATING THIS WITH YOUR MOMMY?

COOKIE IN A MUG

INGREDIENTS

- Granulated sugar
- Brown sugar
- Butter
- Egg yolk
- Vanilla Extract
- Chocolate chips
- Flour
- Salt

DIRECTIONS FOR MOMMY

1 Melt the butter and combine with the 1 tablespoon of each of the sugars listed in a mixing bowl.

2 Add in the egg yolk and vanilla extract.

3 Stir in about 1/4 cup flour and pinch of salt, until fully combined.

DIRECTIONS FOR ME

 4 Fold in the chocolate chips.

 5 Microwave for 1 minute.

6 Serve hot with a scoop of ice cream on top!

WHAT WAS YOUR FAVORITE PART OF CREATING THIS WITH YOUR MOMMY?

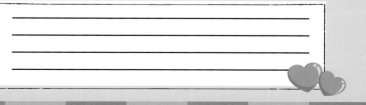

MINI PANCAKE BITES

INGREDIENTS

- Pancake Mix
- Butter
- Spray oil
- Toppings: Strawberries, Blueberries, Chocolate chips, Cinnamon, Bananas, etc.

DIRECTIONS FOR MOMMY

1 Preheat the oven to 350°F.

2 Create your pancake mix according to the package instructions.

3 Oil a mini muffin tin and fill each hole a little over half way with pancake mix.

DIRECTIONS FOR ME

4 Top each mini pancake with your choices of toppings!

5 Cook in the oven for 15-20 minutes.

6 Enjoy!

WHAT WAS YOUR FAVORITE PART OF CREATING THIS WITH YOUR MOMMY?

UNICORN POPCORN

INGREDIENTS

- Sugar
- Butter
- Corn syrup (Optional)
- Salt
- Vanilla Extract
- Popcorn
- Sprinkles

DIRECTIONS FOR MOMMY

1 Heat the sugar, butter, corn syrup, and salt until boiling.

2 Let it boil for 2 minutes, then pour over the popcorn.

3 Stir until popcorn is evenly coated, then fold in the sprinkles.

DIRECTIONS FOR ME

4 Once cool enough, dip your hands in cold water and grab a handful of the popcorn mixture.

5 Form the mixture into balls, about 3 inches, and place on parchment paper.

6 Cover each ball in seran wrap, and tie top with a string to keep.

WHAT WAS YOUR FAVORITE PART OF CREATING THIS WITH YOUR MOMMY?

HOMEMADE FRUIT ROLL UPS

INGREDIENTS

- Strawberries
- Applesauce

DIRECTIONS FOR MOMMY & ME

1. Preheat the oven to 175°F.

2. Wash and cut up your strawberries into large chunks, then add them into a food processor or blender.

3. Blend your strawberries until they are roughly chopped.

4. Add in the applesauce and puree until there are no chunks.

5. Line two cookie sheets with parchment paper and create a thin layer of your mixture on each.

6. Bake for 4 hours, or until your mixture is no longer sticky.

7. Once out of the oven and cooled, cut the parchment paper into strips.

WHAT WAS YOUR FAVORITE PART OF CREATING THIS WITH YOUR MOMMY?

HOMEMADE DONUTS

INGREDIENTS

- Pillsbury Honey Butter Biscuits
- Oil
- Powdered sugar
- Water

DIRECTIONS FOR MOMMY & ME

1. Bring the oil to about 300°F on the stove.
2. Open the can of biscuit dough, and cut a hole out of the center of each biscuit.
3. Then, stretch the donut out a little to make it larger.
4. Place the donut in the oil, one or two at a time.
5. Cook until each side is golden brown.
6. Mix a cup of powdered sugar and a tablespoon of water to create a glaze.
7. Dip the tops of the donuts into the glaze.
8. You can cook the centers of each biscuit as well to make donut holes!

WHAT WAS YOUR FAVORITE PART OF CREATING THIS WITH YOUR MOMMY?

PROTEIN SUSHI

INGREDIENTS

- Tortilla
- Ham/Turkey
- Mayo/Mustard
- Spinach

DIRECTIONS FOR MOMMY

1 On your tortilla, spread mayo or mustard over the entire surface.

4 Roll up your tortilla and cut into bite size pieces.

DIRECTIONS FOR ME

2 Place ham or turkey in the middle of the tortilla.

3 Add any sandwich fixings to the ham or turkey. We add in spinach!

5 Enjoy!

WHAT WAS YOUR FAVORITE PART OF CREATING THIS WITH YOUR MOMMY?

Check out our other book!

MOM, you're the G.O.A.T.

From:

20 Reasons Why You're the Best Mom on Earth

If you enjoyed this book, please leave a 5-star review on Amazon!

Made in the USA
Columbia, SC
28 November 2020